One Word,
many writings

by Adam Francisco

HOLY BIBLE

CONCORDIA PUBLISHING HOUSE · SAINT LOUIS

Copyright © 2012 Concordia Publishing House
3558 S. Jefferson Avenue, St. Louis, MO 63118-3968
1-800-325-3040 • www.cph.org

Written by Adam Francisco

Edited by Mark S. Sengele

Unless otherwise indicated, Scripture quotations are from the ESV Bible® (The Holy Bible, English Standard Version®), copyright © 2001 by Crossway Bibles, a publishing ministry of Good News Publishers. Used by permission. All rights reserved.

Quotations marked *LSB* are from *Lutheran Service Book*, copyright © 2006 Concordia Publishing House. All rights reserved.

Photo credits are found on page 64.

This publication may be available in braille, in large print, or on cassette tape for the visually impaired. Please allow 8 to 12 weeks for delivery. Write to Lutheran Blind Mission, 7550 Watson Rd., St. Louis, MO 63119-4409; call toll-free 1-888-215-2455; or visit the Web site: www.blindmission.org.

Manufactured in the United States of America

Your comments and suggestions concerning the material are appreciated. Please write to Concordia Publishing House, 3558 S. Jefferson Avenue, St. Louis, MO 63118-3968, or contact us at this Web site: youth@cph.org

1 2 3 4 5 6 7 8 9 10   21 20 19 18 17 16 15 14 13 12

Table of Contents

Introduction

Beloved, do not believe every spirit, but test the spirits to see whether they are from God, for many false prophets have gone out into the world. By this you know the Spirit of God: every spirit that confesses that Jesus Christ has come in the flesh is from God, and every spirit that does not confess Jesus is not from God. This is the spirit of the antichrist, which you heard was coming and now is in the world already. Little children, you are from God and have overcome them, for He who is in you is greater than he who is in the world. They are from the world; therefore they speak from the world, and the world listens to them. We are from God. Whoever knows God listens to us; whoever is not from God does not listen to us. By this we know the Spirit of truth and the spirit of error. 1 John 4:1–6

We live in an increasingly interconnected world. We are now able to communicate with people of different cultures with the click of a button. Information is available twenty-four hours a day and seven days a week through the Internet. Traveling overseas is also relatively easy and affordable these days. But you don't have to travel to a different country to experience a different culture. America is a country of considerable cultural and ethnic diversity. Nowhere are these differences more obvious than in the various religions scattered about America's cities and even its rural areas. People of many faiths now live next door to us, work with us, build houses of worship in our neighborhoods, and even find converts among our friends.

One Word, many writings is a Bible study resource created to address this demographic trend. The holy writings of Christianity and other religious faiths are examined and compared, with a goal of identifying the source of each and providing some tools for Christians who encounter people of other faiths in their daily lives. The subjects and the Bible studies in this book are appropriate for high-school-age young people through older adults.

Why Study Other Religious Writings?

Religion is inherent in all cultures and all people. This study then is a study of people and the source of their core beliefs. Undertaking such a study is beneficial for the following reasons:

We may better understand people of other faiths, so that we do not fear or avoid them but are able to interact with them from a base knowledge. We will have "points of contact" from which conversations may arise.

We may grow in compassion for the 3.7 billion people who do not know the one true God. They are people who need the Gospel, who do not know the benefit of God's grace in His Word and Sacraments.

We may be better able to avoid the influence of false religious writings and hold more firmly to our Christian faith. It can be helpful to test the mettle of our convictions against the beliefs of others.

We are not alone. We cannot avoid increased contact with other religions and their writings in the twenty-first century, but we can be prepared for such contact.

We have a compelling need to share Jesus Christ with others. To a world with many gods, we can offer the blessing of faith in the one God who is the only Creator, Redeemer, and Sanctifier of all people. This is a truth that we cannot help but share.

Suggestions for Adapting and Using These Studies

It is not required that all twelve studies in this book be taught or that they be taught in a particular order. While most groups will benefit from reviewing the basic writings of Christianity in Sessions 1 and 2, some may prefer to skip these studies or use them as a conclusion.

If you decide to use only some of the studies initially, consider these points as you make your choices:

What religions are prominent in current events now?

What religions are prominent in your community?

What religions are prominent in the media?

Finally, while these studies will meet the needs of many groups, you may need to alter them in order to make them fit the needs and characteristics of your group.

1

The Old Testament

Lesson Focus

Marcionites—an early second-century heresy—essentially viewed the God of the Old Testament to be different than the one revealed in the New Testament. As Christians, we take all the writings contained in both the Old and New Testaments to be God's revelation. The Old Testament is God's revelation prior to the incarnation of His Son—the Messiah, prophesied from Genesis 3:15. The story continues through the patriarchs, the prophets, and all of ancient Israel's history.

Even so, there are a number of issues raised by modern critics of Christianity concerning the Old Testament. The most prominent are (1) the text of the Old Testament is untrustworthy, as our English translations are based on manuscripts that date back only to the Middle Ages (hundreds of years after the various books were written), and (2) the Christian interpretation of the Old Testament is an erroneous imposition of Christian theology on what is essentially a Jewish book that shapes the covenant laws of Judaism.

(*Note*: Lutheran Hour Ministries has an excellent study, *How We Got the Bible*, available through their Web site lhmmen.com. You may find it useful for both this lesson and the one on the New Testament.)

Opening Discussion

To initiate classroom discussion, ask students the following questions:

What do you know and/or think about the Old Testament, especially in connection to the New Testament? (Some

students may understand the connection between the Testaments, while others may not. Help build their understanding through the rest of this lesson.)

What is your favorite book or historical narrative contained in a book of the Old Testament? Why? (Answers will vary; accept all reasonable responses.)

How is it that Jews, who see the coming of the Messiah as an event that has yet to come, and Christians, who see Jesus as the Messiah, both derive this confession of faith from the Old Testament? Similarly, how is it that both can claim the Old Testament to be the Word of God? (For Judaism, the Hebrew Bible is primarily about the covenant relationship between God and His chosen nation, which is constituted by the Law. For Christianity, the Hebrew Bible is a compilation of books penned by God's people, who looked forward from ancient times to the new covenant God would establish with His people. Both Christianity and Judaism teach that the Old Testament Scriptures were inspired by God and recorded by His faithful prophets and people.)

You may wish to consult Lesson 2 of *One God, many gods* (cph.org, item 20-3406) for a brief synopsis of Judaism and its view of the Old Testament. You can also provide copies of Quick Reference Page 1 for participants.

Understanding the Old Testament

Distribute copies of Participant Page 1. It provides a concise summary of some of the issues surrounding the reliability of the Old Testament text and a basic introduction to the reasons why Christians regard the Old Testament as the inspired Word of God that, at its core, points to the coming of Christ.

After students have had time to read the handout, ask and allow the class (individually or in small groups) to answer the following questions:

The Old Testament is often regarded as one part of the book we call the Bible. Is this really correct? What sort of literature is found in the Old Testament? (The Old Testament is one part of the complete book we call the Holy Bible. At the same time, the Old Testament is considered the Jewish [Hebrew] Bible. It contains historical, prophecy, and wisdom literature with a variety of writing styles.)

The claim is made that the Hebrew Bible Jesus read contained the same text and message as the one in our English Bibles. Is this claim justified even if our Bibles are based on manuscripts that date back to the ninth century at the earliest? Explain your answer. (Jesus references specific accounts or quotes specific words of the Old Testament in His teach-

ing. This is especially seen in the account of Jesus teaching His disciples on the road to Emmaus following the resurrection. While the current translations are based on ninth-century copies, the more recent discovery of older sections of Scripture, such as the Dead Sea Scrolls, has reinforced the accuracy of those ninth-century copies.)

What role does the Old Testament play in Christian theology? (For the Christian, the Old Testament contains not just the Law of God, but more important, the prophecies which point to the coming of the Savior.)

Thinking about the Old Testament

After briefly discussing the Old Testament, have students discuss the questions from the opening discussion again (if necessary), and continue with the following.

Christians often assume the Old Testament is the Word of God. Indeed it is! But there might be a better way to articulate why we hold the Old Testament to be God's very Word. Have the students read Matthew 5:17–19 and John 10:34–35 before addressing the issues concerning whether the Old Testament can be considered God's Word. You may need to explain that when Jesus uses the term *Law*, it is a reference to the whole Hebrew Bible as is made plain by His quotation of Psalm 82:6 in John 10:34. The point here is that God the Son Himself asserted that the Hebrew Bible or Old Testament is and remains authoritative.

Christians also teach that the Old Testament records a number of promises that were fulfilled by Jesus. Is this correct or, as is sometimes claimed, an imposition of Christian theological interpretation on the Old Testament text? Certainly there are good reasons to believe the Christian perspective. If time permits, look at the following specific messianic prophecies:

On Jesus' birth: Micah 5:2; Isaiah 7:13–15

On Jesus' life: Isaiah 35:5–6; 53:3; 61:1

On Jesus' death: Psalm 22:16; Isaiah 53:5–6, 12

On Jesus' resurrection: Psalm 16:10; Isaiah 53:10

Closing

Conclude the study with the following prayer or one of your own.

Almighty God, we thank and praise You for calling us to faith in Your Son. Continue to sustain us in the one true faith, and grant to us the courage to point our neighbors and friends to Jesus. In His name, we pray. Amen.

The Old Testament

The Old Testament is the Christian term for the Jewish (Hebrew) Bible. It comprises thirty-nine books grouped into three major sections. The Torah (or Pentateuch) consists of the first five books and records the creation account, God's covenant with Abraham and the other patriarchs, and the early history of these His chosen people. The Prophets contain books of prophecy or written by prophets. The Writings contain both what is known as Wisdom Literature (e.g., Proverbs and Psalms), as well as historical books (1 and 2 Chronicles), although some historical books are found in the Prophets (Joshua and Judges).

The history of the Old Testament is rather complicated. Indeed, there is much scholarly conjecture on when the books were written and who the authors were. That need not bother us so much (though these are important issues), for what we do know is the Old Testament we have today is the same biblical text Jesus read. Interestingly, though, the copies of and translations made from the Hebrew Bible used from the Middle Ages up to the twentieth century were all based on manuscripts dating at the earliest to the ninth or tenth century AD. (The text from these manuscripts is known as the Masoretic Text.)

So on what basis can Christians be confident that the Old Testament text they read is the same text Jesus read? After all, over eight hundred years have passed between the time of Jesus and the earliest complete compilation of the Hebrew Old Testament. Moreover, the Greek translation of the Old Testament (the Septuagint), which many of the New Testament authors quote, was initially composed between the third and second century BC and includes many slight differences from the Hebrew (mostly accounted for by the differences in language). Skeptics would further add that certainly there must have been some additions, revisions, or perhaps deletions made.

It is true that hundreds of years separate the time of Jesus and the earliest complete copy of the Old Testament, but we have reason to be confident in the text. First, there is no evidence to suggest the text has been corrupted to a point that one should lose confidence in its reliability. Second, and perhaps most significant, biblical manuscripts found among the Dead Sea Scrolls dating to the late-third or early-second century BC confirm—though there are some minor (e.g., orthographic) differences—the reliability of the transmission of the text.

What is so significant about this? This is the Bible Jesus read, but more important, it is the same text He identified as the very Word of God. If God the Son, Jesus Christ, regards it as God's Word, we ought to take the same view. In other words, the Christian view of the inspiration of the Bible—the Old Testament in this case—is not based on merely an assumption but inductive reasoning.

There is another reason why this is important. When Jesus spoke to two of His disciples en route to Emmaus on the day of resurrection, He pointed out that the Old Testament taken as a whole—"Moses and the Prophets," as He put it—point to Him. This vindicates what some refer to as the Christian reading, or Christ-centered interpretation, of the Hebrew Bible.

It is at this point that Judaism and Christianity part ways. For Judaism, the Hebrew Bible is primarily about the covenant relationship between God and His chosen nation, which is constituted by the Law. For Christianity, the Hebrew Bible is ultimately a compilation of books penned by God's people, who looked forward from ancient times to the new covenant God would establish with His people (see Jeremiah 31:31). His promise to crush the work of Satan, first delivered to Adam and Eve (see Genesis 3:15), and continually reiterated throughout the history of His people, would be fulfilled in Jesus.

2
The New Testament

Lesson Focus

The New Testament serves as the primary source for Christian theology. It includes the narrative of Jesus' life, written from four different perspectives; a history of the Early Christian Church and its missionary activity; and the organizing principles that constitute the Christian faith. This session provides just a snapshot of the New Testament with a particular focus on the Gospels.

Opening Discussion

It won't be hard to get a discussion of the New Testament going. This is the part of the Bible that Christians are most familiar with. So begin by asking basic subject questions of the class such as these: What role does the New Testament play in your life as a Christian? What is your favorite portion of the New Testament? Why? (*Note:* Lutheran Hour Ministries has an excellent study, *How We Got the Bible,* available through their Web site: lhmmen.com. You may find it useful for both this lesson and the one on the Old Testament.)

Understanding the New Testament

Distribute copies of Participant Page 2. It provides a concise summary of some of the issues surrounding the reliability of the New Testament's record of Jesus and a basic introduction to the primary theme of the New Testament texts. For further insights on the basics of Christianity, provide copies of Quick Reference Page 2.

After students have had time to read the handout, ask and allow the class (individually or in small groups) to answer the following questions:

> The New Testament is often regarded as one part of the book we call the Bible. Is this really correct? What sort of literature is found in the New Testament? (The New Testament certainly comprises part of what we call the Bible. The literature styles include four biographies, a historical narrative, epistles [letters], and apocalyptic writings.)

> How does the New Testament relate to the Old? (The New Testament reveals the fulfillment of the prophecies found in the Old Testament.)

> What are some of the different points of emphasis in the four Gospels? If they all claim to be records of Jesus' life, why do they report things differently? (Each of the Gospels presents the account of the life of Christ from the author's unique perspective. Matthew's account was written to a Jewish audience. Mark's active account would appeal to a Greek/Roman audience. Luke's detailed account reflects his advanced education. John's account collects the sayings and miracles of Jesus.)

> What role does the New Testament play in Christian theology? (Our theology is formed by the contents of the New Testament.)

Thinking about the New Testament

After briefly discussing the basic issues surrounding the New Testament, have students discuss the following questions:

It is often claimed that while the four Gospels of the New Testament are ancient sources on the life of Jesus, there are other ancient texts that record a very different picture of Jesus. Ask the students if they know of any of these so-called noncanonical gospels. (A list with links to various texts can

be found at wesley.nnu.edu/sermons-essays-books/noncanonical-literature/noncanonical-literature-gospels.) Then ask the class to discuss why only the Gospels of Matthew, Mark, Luke, and John are regarded as authoritative.

The answer lies in the fact that these are the only Gospels written by people in a position to write about the historical Jesus, as the writers were eyewitnesses or companions of eyewitnesses to the life of Christ. Additionally, what could be said of these texts and others written by or confirmed by the apostles? Direct the students to discuss this. Then ask them to read the following passages from the Gospel of John: 14:26–27 and 16:12–15. What are the implications of Jesus' words?

The message the apostles would preach would be attended by the Holy Spirit. This same message would be recorded in the various texts of the New Testament. What about Paul? He was not present when Jesus delivered the promise of apostolic inspiration to the apostles. The answer can be found in two places. First, in the Book of Acts, Paul is clearly viewed as teaching in accord with the apostles, and, second, his letters are given the status of Scripture by the apostolic church (see 2 Peter 3:15).

Not only are the Gospels reliable records of history, but they—and the rest of the New Testament—are also inspired by God the Holy Spirit. All of the New Testament is, in one way or another, about Jesus Christ and the victory He won (for us) on Calvary. That is certainly clear in the Gospels and the preaching of the apostles in Acts. In conclusion, ask the students to reflect on the Book of Revelation or a favorite epistle and relate that text to Christ and the doctrine of justification by grace through faith in Him alone.

Closing

Conclude the study with the following prayer from the inside of *Lutheran Service Book* or one of your own.

Lord God, bless Your Word wherever it is proclaimed. Make it a power and peace to convert those not yet Your own and to confirm those who have come to saving faith. May Your Word pass from the ear to the heart, from the heart to the lip, and from the lip to the life that, as You have promised, Your Word may achieve the purpose for which You send it; through Jesus Christ, our Lord. Amen.

The New Testament

The New Testament is, along with the Old, the Christian Scripture. It is not just one book. Rather, it comprises twenty-seven first-century writings by a handful of authors, all of which—in one way or another—bear witness to the fact that God was, in Christ, reconciling the world unto Himself (2 Corinthians 5:19).

The first four books are the Gospels. These are biographical accounts of Jesus' life that were written by eyewitnesses of His life (in the case of Matthew and John), as well as companions of eyewitnesses. (Mark recorded Peter's account, and Luke recorded the account of Paul [see Luke 1:1–4]). The texts of the Gospels in the early manuscripts don't exactly tell us who wrote them, however. So the question often arises concerning how we know that the names now affixed to them really reflect who wrote them. While the answer is often complicated by scholars, the bottom line (and the simplest explanation) is that early extrabiblical material, dating to the late-first and into the second century indicate as much. (See *The Lutheran Study Bible*, pp. 1573–74.)

Why is this important? There are a number of reasons. Probably most important is that many popular authors on Christianity try to discredit the authority of the four Gospels by alleging they were only chosen as authoritative because they supported a particular understanding of Jesus over against other gospels (see Lesson 3 on The Gospel of Thomas). That the Gospels were written by eyewitnesses of Jesus' life and those whose account came from eyewitness sources and would have been checked for accuracy against the testimony of eyewitnesses makes all the difference. Only they—and not authors writing under pseudonyms in later centuries (as is the case with noncanonical gospels)—were in the position to accurately record the life of Jesus.

Skeptics nevertheless often draw attention to the fact that the four Gospels do not agree on the details of Jesus' life. How, then, can they be regarded as reliable? The answer has to do with the intent of the author. The Gospel writers were not writing biographies as we think of them today. They were writing biographies in the tradition of the Greco-Roman world where the author used literature to convince their audience of something. The Gospel writers were clear: they wrote to convince their readers that Jesus was the Messiah, the Son of the living God, sent to save sinners by atoning for their sins (see Matthew 16:13–16; Mark 10:45; Luke 1:1–4, 24:45–49; and John 20:30–31). The differences found between the Gospels are a result of each author's attempt to appeal to a certain audience. It's not that they made material up; in fact, decade after decade, the Gospels continually prove to match up with the historical and archeological record. (On this, see Paul L. Maier, *In the Fullness of Time*.)

Following the Gospels is the Book of Acts, the earliest record of the growth of the Christian Church. It is, according to Luke (its author) in the opening verses, a continuation of his Gospel. But Acts is also more than a historical narrative. It records for us the essential message of Christianity as it was carried forth by the apostles: that Jesus is the Christ, who, through His death and resurrection, fulfilled the testimony of "all the prophets" (3:24) and did so not in some unverifiable realm of history, but publicly for all to see (see 26:26). Acts is followed by a number of epistles (letters) written by Paul, Peter, John, and others that, in response to various situations, continue to detail the content of the Christian faith, all of which revolves around and is held together by Jesus Christ (Colossians 1:17). The last book of the New Testament is Revelation. It is also one of the most misunderstood books of the New Testament. This is largely due to its symbolism and the fact that it points to events that are yet to come. The point of it and, one could argue, the whole New Testament, however, is that the promised offspring of a woman, who would destroy the work of Satan and the effects it has had on creation (sin and death), came in the person and work of Jesus and is continuing to be realized through the work of the Holy Spirit.

3

The Gospel of Thomas

Lesson Focus

A considerable amount of attention has been given to various ancient texts which reportedly describe the life and teachings of Jesus in a manner that contradicts the biblical Gospels. The Gospel of Thomas is the most famous of these texts. Some scholars even regard it as equal in authority to the Gospels of Matthew, Mark, Luke, and John. These opinions present a challenge for Christians who may encounter the claims of the Gospel of Thomas, as well as the claims of some scholars.

Opening Discussion

Begin by asking students if they have heard of the Gospel of Thomas. Some may have even read part of the text. Ask those participants acquainted with the Gospel of Thomas to share their perceptions of the text (and perhaps others similar to it). Allow participants to express viewpoints, but keep this discussion time to a minimum. Bring it to a close by making the point that texts such as the Gospel of Thomas and other noncanonical gospels are accepted by some critical Bible scholars. It is therefore important to know why historic Christianity rejects the authority of these texts.

Understanding the Gospel of Thomas

Distribute copies of Participant Page 3; it provides a concise summary of the background and content of the Gospel of Thomas.

After allowing students time to read the handout, allow them to discuss the information provided. Then discuss as a class or in small groups the following questions:

What is the Gospel of Thomas? (A collection of writings, reported to be about Christ, but not part of the recognized biblical accounts)

Where and when was it discovered? (The Gospel of Thomas was discovered in 1945, along with a host of other ancient texts, in Egypt not far from Cairo at a place called Nag Hammadi.)

When was it probably written? (Probably around the end of the second century)

How does the Gospel of Thomas compare to the four Gospels? (It was not recorded by an eyewitness. It does not record the story of Christ's life and ministry; rather it contains a collection of supposed "hidden sayings" of Jesus.)

What do you think is most interesting about the Gospel of Thomas? (Answers will vary.)

Thinking about the Gospel of Thomas

After discussing the text of the Gospel of Thomas, ask students how they think it should be regarded? (You may want to peruse it at sacred-texts.com/chr/thomas.htm, or obtain a printed copy from your local library or bookstore.) (While interesting reading, the Gospel of Thomas is not part of the biblical text; it should be considered fiction rather than a true account of the words of Jesus.)

Emphasize the point that the Gospel of Thomas (and every other noncanonical gospel) was written a century and a half or more after Jesus walked the earth. In other words, it was not written by eyewitnesses or companions of eyewitnesses.

Conversely, ask them why they think the Gospels of Matthew, Mark, Luke, and John alone should be considered authoritative on the life of Jesus over against the Gospel of Thomas and others writings like it.

The biblical Gospels were written by men who knew Jesus personally and saw Him after His resurrection (Matthew and John) and those who were close confidants of the apostles (Mark and Luke). Moreover, all four are connected directly (in the case of Matthew and John) and indirectly (in the case of Mark and Luke) to Jesus.

Read John 14:16; 14:26; and 16:13. What further promise does Jesus give concerning the words of these writers? How should this affect the way we view the Scriptures? (Jesus' promises that what the apostles would preach and teach [and write] would be inspired by the Holy Spirit. Christians can be confident in not only the historical legitimacy of the canonical Gospels, but also their divine inspiration.)

Closing

Conclude the study with the following prayer or one of your own.

Heavenly Father, You have caused the Holy Gospels to be written so that we might know all that You accomplished for us and our salvation through Your Son. We thank You that the Gospels were written down and preserved through the ages in the writings of Matthew, Mark, Luke, and John. Keep us ever mindful of all You have done for us, and keep us ever attentive to Your Word. Amen.

The Gospel of Thomas

The Gospel of Thomas is the most famous writing in a group of texts known generally as the noncanonical gospels (i.e., accounts of Jesus' words and deeds not found in the New Testament). Like the other noncanonical texts, it was not written by an eyewitness of Jesus' life or a companion of an eyewitness (despite its title). It was probably written, recent scholarship attests, toward the end of the second century AD.

The Gospel of Thomas was discovered in 1945, along with a host of other ancient texts, in Egypt not far from Cairo at a place called Nag Hammadi. It was translated into English in 1977, and continues to attract a tremendous amount of attention, as it challenges some of the core teachings of the New Testament.

It does not purport to narrate the life of Jesus. In fact, none of His deeds—the miracles He performed, His fulfillment of Messianic prophecy, crucifixion, or resurrection—are mentioned. Instead, it claims to record the secret or "hidden sayings" of Jesus in 114 sections. Around half of what the author recorded coheres with what the eyewitnesses and their companions recorded in the New Testament. The rest, however, challenges the Good News of salvation by grace through faith in Christ and His death for our sins and resurrection for our justification.

For example, the Jesus found in the Gospel of Thomas teaches a sort of mysticism. Salvation is not the result of God's activity on our behalf through His Son; instead, it is attained through knowledge. What keeps humans from reaching their spiritual potential and, perhaps, reaching God, is their materialism and the distractions of this world. Such knowledge is only attained through a personal introspection. Saying 70, for example, records Jesus as saying, "If you bring forth what is within you, what you bring forth will save you."

Overall, Jesus is not a savior in the Gospel of Thomas. He is more of a spiritual sage who says in saying 77, "It is I who am the light which is above them all. It is I who am the All. From Me did the All come forth, and unto Me did the All extend. Split a piece of wood, and I am there. Lift up the stone, and you will find Me there." Even more strange, in saying 114, He says, "Every woman who will make herself male will enter the Kingdom of Heaven."

Despite this, there are skeptics of Christianity who regard the Gospel of Thomas as equal in authority to the New Testament Gospels. Some have even asserted that, due to its similarities as well as disparities with the New Testament, it predates—and perhaps was a source for—the Gospels of Matthew, Mark, Luke, and John. Contemporary scholars, however, have shown that the Gospel of Thomas was written late in the second century at the earliest and therefore cannot be considered a reliable account of Jesus' words.

Note: There are a number of translations of the Gospel of Thomas in print as well as on the Internet (e.g., see sacred-texts.com/chr/thomas.htm).

4

The Qur'an

Lesson Focus

Islam may be the fastest growing religion in the world. Despite its prominent place in public discourse, it nevertheless remains largely misunderstood. Many people seem to have an opinion about what constitutes the true teachings of Islam, and many of the teachings are contradictory. This lesson looks at Islam's central text, the Qur'an, from which the essential teachings of Islam are derived and by which the Muslim worldview is shaped.

Opening Discussion

Begin by asking students if they have read the Qur'an or portions of it. This might cause a bit of discomfort, for some Christians maintain reading such a book—filled with what amount to false claims about God—might be dangerous for Christians.

This has been an issue throughout the history of Christianity and its approach to Islam. It was even an issue in Martin Luther's day. Luther, however, was confident that Christians absolutely needed to be aware of Islam and its teachings. Not only did Luther encourage the study of the Qur'an, but he also wrote an introduction for it, which was included in the first publication of a Latin translation of the Muslim holy book in 1543. In fact, it was a Lutheran pastor named Salomon Schweigger who first translated the Qur'an into German in 1616.

Next, ask those participants who are acquainted with the Qur'an what their perceptions of the text are. Allow students to express their viewpoints, but keep this time of discussion to a minimum. Bring it to a close by making the point that if a Christian is to talk reasonably and honestly about Islam and its teachings (and perhaps to dialogue with Muslims), they must ensure their conversation is based on facts and texts rather than perceptions and emotions.

Understanding the Qur'an

Distribute copies of Participant Page 4. It provides a concise summary of what Muslims think about the Qur'an, how they understand and interpret it, and what it teaches. To provide more information on Islam for participants, provide copies of Quick Reference Page 4. You may also want to consult Lesson 3 of *One God, many gods* (cph.org, item 20-3406).

After students have had a chance to read the handout, allow them to discuss what they have read. Then ask and have the class (individually or in small groups) answer the following questions:

How did the Qur'an come to be written? (According to Muslim tradition, the Qur'an was put together in a definitive edition around AD 650, about two decades after Muhammad [c. 570–632], the prophet of Islam, died.)

What is the nature of the Qur'an, according to the Muslim mind? (An overwhelming majority of Muslims regard it as the eternal speech of God enshrined in a written text. Its content is viewed as being the perfectly transcribed words that God spoke—and continues to speak—through Muhammad.)

In terms of ascertaining the definitive teachings of the Qur'an, how do Muslims approach the text of the Qur'an? (The principles revealed through the Qur'an are more than just theological. They also incorporate legal tenets.)

What is the character of Islam, according to the Qur'an? (All of it, including Muhammad's moral example, are viewed as the perfect religion for humanity [Qur'an 5:3] and is to be advanced throughout the world until Islam prevails over all other religions [9:33] through a political, military, and missiological struggle [jihad] until the day that God judges the living and the dead.)

Thinking about the Teachings of the Qur'an

After discussing the text of the Qur'an, ask students how they think the Qur'an should be regarded? (You may want to peruse the Qur'an at sacred-texts.com/isl/htq/index.htm, or

obtain your own copy.) Is it a text that perhaps could be used for discussion with a Muslim as Christians seek ways to address the spiritual needs of Muslims? (Allow students to share their thoughts and ideas.)

There are different ways of thinking about this. Paul, for example, quoted pagan texts as a springboard for his Gospel proclamation at Mars Hill in Acts 17. Some missionaries to Muslims use seemingly contradictory passages from the Qur'an to point out the issue that whether or not Jesus died and rose again needs to be resolved by texts written closer to the time of Jesus (e.g., by reading the eyewitnesses Matthew and John or the companions of Peter and Paul, that is, Mark and Luke). An example of such contradictory passages compares Qur'an 19:33 (where it appears that Jesus " . . . shall be raised up to life") and Qur'an 4:157 (where Jesus' crucifixion and, by extension, His resurrection are denied). The Qur'an, however, is intrinsically hostile to creedal Christianity, envisioning Christian teaching as a product of historical innovation. In this regard, others have cautioned against using the Qur'an in outreach to Muslims. It is hard to say what the best approach might be. The context of the Christian and Muslim in dialogue will have to determine the best approach.

Read Acts 17:16–31. How could Paul's approach to the people of Athens serve as a model to our approach to Muslims? (Answers will vary. Focus on positive ways to engage followers of Islam in faith discussions.) You may want to bring a close to your discussion by asking how the class should think about the Qur'an and how they might respond when asked how it should be regarded. There is indeed much to say about the Qur'an. Scholars and laypeople fill the Internet and books with information and arguments about its history, teachings, and legacy. At the bottom of it all, Christians should understand that the Qur'an views itself (as do Muslims) as a book filled with teachings given by God to replace the alleged corrupted Bible and teachings of Christianity.

Closing

Conclude the study with the following prayer or one of your own.

Heavenly Father, we thank You that we can rest assured in the accomplished fact of our salvation through the death and resurrection of Your Son, Jesus Christ. Keep us ever mindful of this through the power of the Holy Spirit, and give us courage to address the challenges posed by the growth of Islam and wisdom in our approach toward Muslim people. Amen.

The Qur'an

The Qur'an is the sacred book of Islam. An overwhelming majority of Muslims regard it as the eternal speech of God enshrined in a written text. The Qur'an acknowledges that there have been other scriptures, such as the Torah, Psalms, and Gospel, revealed by God through prophets. These are, however, deemed by Muslims as corrupt. As such, only the Qur'an remains authoritative.

According to Muslim tradition, the Qur'an was put together in a definitive edition around AD 650, about two decades after Muhammad (c. 570–632), the prophet of Islam, died. Its content, nevertheless, was viewed as being the perfectly transcribed words that God spoke—and continues to speak—through Muhammad.

One of the more curious characteristics about the Qur'an is that it is not chronological. In other words, it wasn't put together the way Muhammad allegedly communicated his messages. A close reading of an annotated version of the Qur'an reveals that much of what comes at the front of the book is dated to the later part of Muhammad's life, whereas the shorter chapters—or suras—found at the end are recognized as having been uttered during the beginning of Muhammad's career.

Contradictions also exist within the text of the Qur'an. For example, in one verse, it praises the consumption of wine (16:67); elsewhere consuming wine is prohibited (5:90–91). In another verse, Muslims are instructed to treat Christians and Jews with respect (29:46); elsewhere Muslims are instructed to harm them (9:29). How are these contradictions resolved? Following Qur'an 2:106 and other passages like it, Muslim theologians have asserted that God progressively revealed Himself throughout the course of Muhammad's life such that God abrogates (cancels out) early revelations with later ones. (Therefore, Qur'an 5:90–91 abrogates 16:67, and 9:29 abrogates 29:46.)

Despite its complexities, the narrative of the Qur'an can be summarized fairly briefly. It teaches that at a certain point, God created the heavens and the earth, the seen and the unseen. The first humans, Adam and his female consort (who is not named in the Qur'an) disobeyed God and were punished by being cast down from a heavenly paradise to earth. Their sin was immediately pardoned and did not tarnish them or their offspring.

To provide clear guidance to humans so they would know exactly what was right and wrong, the Qur'an claims God has raised up a large number of prophets throughout the course of human history beginning with Adam and extending through Moses, David, and Jesus, terminating with Muhammad. It is the revelation given through Muhammad that brings to an end the lineage of the prophets. The Qur'an also corrects the message of all the former prophets, for it has been corrupted and ignored by humankind.

The principles revealed through Muhammad were more than just theological. They also incorporated legal tenets. All of Islam, including Muhammad's moral example, is viewed as the perfect religion for humanity (Qur'an 5:3) and is to be advanced throughout the world until Islam prevails over all other religions (9:33) through a political, military, and missiological struggle (jihad) until the day that God judges the living and the dead.

Note: There are a number of translations of the Qur'an in print as well as on the Internet (e.g., sacred-texts.com/isl/htq/index.htm).

5

The Analects of Confucius

Lesson Focus

Confucius was a late-sixth and early-fifth century BC Chinese sage. Confucianism, a belief system based on his teachings, pervades much of Chinese thought and culture. A study of Confucius' Analects is thus a window into one of China's most fundamental philosophies. This is beneficial in its own right given China's rising stature in the world. For the Christian who has or will have Chinese friends or colleagues, it is also vital for any evangelical possibilities that may come to pass.

Opening Discussion

Begin by asking students if they have heard of Confucianism and its most fundamental text—The Analects. If any have, let them share what they know. You may want to consult Lesson 8 of *One God, many gods* (cph.org, item 20-3406) to help guide the discussion.

Much controversy exists regarding whether The Analects constitutes a religious text or not. Whatever the case, its teachings grip the mind of the Chinese. While it is true that the larger theological worldview presumed by Confucianism is at odds with a biblical worldview, it is also true that The Analects presents some ideas not entirely at odds with the values of Christianity.

It is possible that The Analects could be used as a connecting point for Christian conversation with minds informed by Confucianism. This conviction guides this study.

Understanding the Analects

Distribute copies of Participant Page 5. It provides a concise summary of the core ideas of The Analects. For additional information on Confucianism and Taoism, provide copies of Quick Reference Page 5/6.

After students have had time to read the handout, allow them to discuss the information provided. Then ask and allow the class (individually or in small groups) to answer the following questions:

For what purpose was The Analects written? (The Analects attempts to address how humans should order their lives.)

Did anything about The Analects surprise you? (Accept all reasonable answers.)

The Analects is much more sociopolitical than theological in nature. Since it deals more with the horizontal relationships of humans, are there any points of Confucianism a Christian might find useful for conversation with those who are part of the Confucian tradition? (As Christians, we can approach the follower of Confucianism by addressing the positive life values addressed in both faith traditions.)

Thinking about the Teachings of The Analects

After briefly discussing The Analects, have students read and reflect on Romans 2:14–15. (Copies of The Analects are available online at sacred-texts.com/cfu/conf1.htm, or obtain a copy at your local library or bookstore.) What implications do Paul's words have for Christians in their dealings with non-Christians?

Christians should not be surprised that people from radically dissimilar cultures, who view things very differently than we do, have some inherent recognition that there are certain ethical standards not unlike our own. It could be argued that the ethical impulse in The Analects is an expression of that law of God—that says we should treat others as we would be treated, for example—written on the human heart.

Obviously there is much in Confucianism—particu-

larly its broader animistic and, perhaps, polytheistic worldview—that is problematic (and false). But at the same time, there is much in the teachings of The Analects that could be used to push beyond idle conversation to a dialogue about the fundamental problem of humanity—that we know what we ought to do but never do it.

Ask students to answer the following question again: Are there any points of Confucianism a Christian might find useful for conversation with those who are part of the Confucian tradition? Follow this up by discussing how the Law illuminates our sinfulness and how its resolution can only be found in the Gospel.

Closing

Conclude the study with the following prayer or one of your own.

Heavenly Father, You have made all men and women. You have commanded us to live together in service to one another. And yet we fail. We fail miserably. Even so, You still love us. You love all of Your creation so much that You sent Your only Son to die for the sins of the world. We thank You and ask that You would grant us the zeal to be Your witnesses to all that might see and know us. Amen.

The Analects of Confucius

Confucianism is one of China's oldest and most resilient philosophies. Although primarily concerned with political and ethical order, it is underpinned by a broad religious worldview that sees the universe as an orderly cosmos, yet one that is also filled with spirits and deities.

The chief source of Confucian values is a work entitled The Analects. It is essentially a collection of aphorisms (proverbs) attributed to the Chinese sage Confucius (c. 551–479 BC) that was published sometime during China's turbulent Warring States Period (475–221 BC).

It is comprised of twenty chapters, all of which exhibit no real systematic order. In fact, the sequence of the chapters and sayings within them could be said to be compiled in a completely random manner. Nevertheless, there are some key themes that emerge throughout the entire work.

The basic question The Analects attempts to address is how humans should order their lives. How it answers is rather basic. Confucius seems to view all human life and activity as covering three realms. These realms could be illustrated as concentric circles, with family being at the center, communities of families (neighborhoods, villages, or towns) around it, and the state and national government on the outside.

For these three spheres of existence to be properly ordered and remain ordered, they must be guided and supported by three primary virtues. The first and primary virtue is filial piety (*xiao*) or respect and reverence for one's parents and elders. Respect takes the form of reverence, as dead ancestors are venerated and perhaps worshiped in Confucianism.

The second essential virtue in The Analects is *ren*. This is often translated as humaneness, goodness, or benevolence. It revolves around the concept of reciprocity, whereby one acts toward others in the manner one would like to be treated.

The third core virtue is ritualistic propriety (*li*). Another way of thinking about it is the perpetuation of traditions and ceremonies of all sorts. Whether it be religious, political, or familial, maintaining the ways of the ancestors was integral to the strengthening and preservation of the sociopolitical order.

Some scholars refer to these three virtues as the Confucian tripod. This description is appropriate, for The Analects regards these as the fabric that held earthly affairs in order. In doing so, one senses that Confucius believed that it was only when this was achieved that one could approach heaven. In the eleventh chapter of The Analects, Confucius expresses that one can only serve the gods and spirits once one learns to serve his or her neighbor. To be sure, The Analects does not elaborate on the relationship between humans and the divine. Passing references, however, indicate that Confucianism is animistic (it sees the world as teeming with spirits) and perhaps even polytheistic (belief in the existence of many gods) as well.

Despite its peculiarities, particularly for a Christian reader, The Analects remains a tremendously influential text for the Chinese. It is no exaggeration that it has shaped the culture and social philosophy of China for more than two thousand years.

Note: There are a number of translations of The Analects in print as well as on the Internet (e.g., see sacred-texts.com/cfu/conf1.htm).

6

The Tao te Ching

YIN YANG

Lesson Focus

Taoism along (and often blended) with Confucianism pervades much of Chinese thought and culture. A study of its fundamental text—the Tao te Ching—provides a window into one of China's most trenchant philosophies and will aid Christians for any conversations they might have with people of Chinese descent.

Opening Discussion

Begin by asking students if they have heard of Taoism and its most fundamental text—the Tao te Ching. If any have, let them share what they know. You may want to consult Lesson 8 of *One God, many gods* (cph.org, item 20-3406) to help guide the discussion.

Chances are that if students have never heard of the Tao te Ching, they have at least heard of the concepts of *yin* and *yang*. They have probably seen the sign of the yin and yang fused together in a circle (the *taijitu*), perhaps at the local martial arts studio or on a T-shirt design. Ask students what they think the yin and yang represent.

Some discussion on the complementary forces that are at work in the world will probably (or at least should) ensue. The Taoist seeks to find himself or herself moved by these forces rather than working against them. This path of least resistance to the unseen forces at work in the world is called the *Tao* or "way." It is this which the Tao te Ching attempts to express.

Understanding the Tao te Ching

Distribute copies of Participant Page 6. It provides a concise summary of the core ideas of the Tao te Ching. For additional information on Taoism and Confucianism, provide copies of Quick Reference Page 5/6.

After students have had time to read the handout, allow them to discuss what they learned. Then ask and allow the class to answer the following questions:

When was the Tao te Ching probably written? (No one really knows when it was composed or who wrote it. Its authorship is usually attributed to an ancient Chinese sage named Lao Zu [Laozi] who may have lived around 500 BC.)

Why is the Tao te Ching popular? (Many attribute the popularity of the Tao te Ching in China and throughout the world to its uncanny ability to lead to a wide variety of interpretations.)

What are the two dominant themes of the Tao te Ching? (First, human beings and the languages that we use are inadequate for describing what is real. Second, knowledge of the "way" is not as important as merely abiding by it.) What surprised you about these themes? (Answers will vary.)

Is there anything in the Tao te Ching that struck you as useful for Christians? (The concept of human language being inadequate to describe the truth of God is certainly one we can relate to as Christians. Yet, while Taoism may seem to answer some questions about the world, its basic teachings are in contradiction to Christianity.)

Thinking about the Teachings of the Tao te Ching

After briefly discussing the Tao te Ching, ask a student to read John 14:6. (You can find the Tao online at sacred-texts.com/tao/taote.htm, or obtain a copy at your local library or bookstore.) Ask him or her how the truth expressed in this verse about the

"way" might compare to the way articulated in the Tao te Ching. (Jesus asserts that He is the only way to the Father; the Tao would offer many paths.)

In Acts 17:26–27, Paul speaks about the order in the world as something God designed so that men and women, in observing it, would seek Him. Ask the class the following questions: In what sense is the Tao te Ching's encouragement to its readers to seek after the "way" confirmation of what Paul talks about in Acts 17? How does the Tao te Ching, by its own admission, fall short of this? How might Christ be the answer to those seeking the Tao?

While Taoism falls seriously (one might say damnably) short of offering any real way of living with any sort of confidence in the future, its admonition that there is a way that one ought to live testifies yet again to the Law written on the heart of each and every human being. In light of this, ask students how they might be able to use the ideas in the Tao te Ching to communicate the person and work of Christ for those seeking the "way" through the Gospel.

Closing

Conclude the study with the following prayer or one of your own.

Lord Jesus Christ, You are the way, the truth, and the light. No one will receive eternal life but through You. Thank You for firmly implanting in our hearts the knowledge of salvation through faith in You. Grant us the courage to take this wonderful message of Your work for us on the cross of Calvary to all of those we encounter. Amen.

The Tao te Ching

The Tao te Ching, or sometimes Dao de Jing, is one of the world's most esoteric theological writings. No one really knows when it was composed or who wrote it. Its authorship is usually attributed to an ancient Chinese sage Lao Zu (Laozi), who may have lived around 500 BC. Scholars continue to debate these matters today. Nevertheless, just as The Analects has shaped Chinese social philosophy for over two thousand years, the Tao te Ching has influenced its larger worldview for just as long.

Is there a Taoist worldview? Perhaps not. The Tao te Ching itself, in its first verse, acknowledges the ineffable (i.e., indescribable) nature of its teachings. Throughout all eighty-one of its verses, one encounters a number of what seem to be strange and contradictory or at least paradoxical ideas. In fact, many attribute the popularity of the Tao te Ching in China and throughout the world to its uncanny ability to lead to a wide variety of interpretations.

Scholars specializing in the Tao te Ching suggest that there are two major points to the text. One has to do with the nature of human language, particularly as it attempts to describe things (such as God) that are beyond comprehension. Human beings and the languages that we use are inadequate for describing what is truly real. By using language, we impose categories and meaning on what we perceive and thereby limit our understanding of reality. If that is the case with the real physical world, the Tao te Ching suggests that it is even more so the case with that which is not perceivable through the senses.

Even so, the Tao te Ching at times explains that humans may perhaps know the way things are in the seen and unseen world. Knowledge of the "way," however, is not as important as merely abiding by it. In fact, one really has no choice. Verse 31 of the Tao te Ching says that even the finest warrior is defeated when he goes against the Tao.

This is the second major theme in the Tao te Ching. The way things are is guided by the Tao. This is the mystery and, as verse 16 puts it, great truth of nature. There is a sense of there being a real natural law in the Tao te Ching. Yet, the Tao is not something placed in nature by an external being or God. It is, in the conception of the Tao te Ching, the driving force of nature.

The Tao te Ching may leave much room for interpretation. It is, nevertheless, rather adverse to the worldview of Christianity, for it has no regard for a Creator much less a Savior. So, while the Tao te Ching may seem aloof to the claims of Christianity, it is actually quite opposed to it.

Note: There are a number of translations of the Tao te Ching in print as well as on the Internet (e.g., see sacred-texts.com/tao/taote.htm).

7

The Lotus Sutra

Lesson Focus

Buddhism is the third major religion—alongside Confucianism and Taoism—in China. It is also prevalent throughout the rest of eastern Asia and has established itself in parts of the western world too. A study of the Lotus Sutra, one of the most fundamental texts in the Buddhist canon, is thus a window into an influential global religious philosophy.

Opening Discussion

Begin class by asking students about Buddhism. Do you know any Buddhists? What do you know about Buddhism? You may want to consult Lesson 5 of *One God, many gods* (cph.org, item 20-3406) to aid in any discussion that may ensue. To provide additional information on the basic teachings of Buddhism for participants, provide copies of Quick Reference Page 7.

Close this discussion by pointing out that there are many forms of Buddhism. Mahayana Buddhism is one of the more pervasive branches. If students know any Buddhists, chances are they come from one of the many branches of the Mahayana school. The Lotus Sutra, a description of which they are about to read, is the most influential text in the Buddhist canon.

Understanding the Lotus Sutra

Distribute copies of Participant Page 7. It provides a concise summary of the core ideas of the Lotus Sutra. After students have had time to read the handout, ask and allow them individually or in small groups to answer the following questions:

What is a *sutra*? (A *sutra* is a sermon or a discourse.)

What is significant about the Lotus Sutra in the context of global Buddhism? (The Lotus Sutra is one of the most important texts for a branch of Buddhism generally known as Mahayana Buddhism. This is the form of Buddhism that grips all of East Asia and is practiced widely in the United States.)

What do you find surprising about the teachings of the Lotus Sutra? (Accept all reasonable answers. The concept that nothing in the world is actually real; it is all merely part of our mind.)

Thinking about the Lotus Sutra

After briefly discussing the Lotus Sutra, have students read and reflect on Genesis 1:1–2:3. (An online version of the Lotus Sutra is available at sacred-texts.com/bud/lotus/index.htm, or obtain a copy at your local library or bookstore.) Ask students to compare and contrast the Lotus Sutra's view of time and space with the biblical account.

Trying to reconcile the creation account is perhaps one of the greatest challenges any Christian—or someone with a western mind-set—will face in dealing with a religion such as Buddhism. The Lotus Sutra doesn't really regard the world that we live in as real space where human actions have real consequences. For the Christian, the reality of sin has grave implications for the person facing a holy and just God. This teaching has no meaning for the entrenched Buddhist.

Next, ask the class what sort of hope the Buddhist in the Mahayana tradition might have in this life as he or she looks to the next. Buddhists find hope in working and thinking their way to enlightenment. If they are incapable of doing this for themselves,

they engage teachers (*bodhisattvas*) who help them along the way. This provides some hope that eventually—either in this life or the next—the Buddhist will achieve nirvana.

These are, of course, false hopes. They can therefore be used as points of discussion between the Christian and the Buddhist. Ask students how they might approach Buddhists with the Gospel. The point to emphasize here is that Buddhists recognize that there is something wrong with our basic existence that must be rectified. They certainly have a different idea of what might be wrong, but this point of agreement offers a chance for the Christian to speak the Gospel to the Buddhist.

The focus should, of course, be on Jesus, who is not only a *great* teacher, but also the *only* teacher who offers a certain solution for our basic existential problems. He is, in fact, the only one who in real time and space came from beyond the empirical realm—and did so in a verifiable way, ultimately demonstrating His divinity by rising from the dead—not to point us to the right path toward enlightenment, but to restore us to a right relationship with God. In addition, God graciously gives us the Holy Spirit, who enlightens us with His gifts and works in us a saving and certain trust that the Creator of the universe loves, sustains, and will always be with us. Finally, we have the promise of life with God eternally.

Closing

Conclude the study with the following prayer or one of your own.

Heavenly Father, You know how fallen we and all men and women across all time and cultures are. Yet, in Your mercy, You decided from the time that sin entered the world that You would send Your Son to teach us what is true. Your Son was not just a great teacher, but He is also a great Savior who, knowing our weakness, accomplished our salvation for us by dying on a cross for our sin and rising from the dead for our justification. We thank You, and ask that You embolden us by Your Spirit to bear witness to Your Son to all we encounter. Amen.

The Lotus Sutra

The Lotus Sutra is one of the most important texts for a branch of Buddhism generally known as Mahayana Buddhism. This is the form of Buddhism that grips all of East Asia and is practiced widely in the United States. The full title of this influential text is *The Sutra of the Lotus Blossom of the Marvelous Dharma*.

No one knows for certain when the Lotus Sutra was composed. Some scholars have suggested that it was first composed somewhere north of the Indian subcontinent during the first century BC. It was nevertheless introduced into China, Korea, and Japan beginning in the late-fourth or early-fifth century AD.

A *sutra* is a sermon or a discourse. Accordingly, the Lotus Sutra is regarded as a compilation of the definitive teachings of Siddhartha Gautama (c. 563–483 BC), the Buddha. Interestingly, however, the text does not contain much content. One scholar has commented that it reads like a long preface without a book.

Further confusing matters, already in the opening chapters of the book, one realizes that much of what is discussed and the beings (humans, nonhumans, and heavenly creatures) described didn't actually take place or exist in history. In fact, the work seems to make the implicit point that time and space as we know it isn't truly real. This is indeed one of the basic tenets of Buddhism: that the world outside our minds (extramental reality, as philosophers call it) doesn't really exist as we think it does.

There is a greater, yet more sublime reality, and it is only realized by a self-conscious awareness of the Four Noble Truths:

- Life is suffering.
- Suffering is a result of craving or attachment to the world we think we perceive but really only exists as a construct of our minds.
* To eliminate suffering, we must eliminate our cravings for and attachment to the illusory world.

- The way to do this is to follow the Eightfold Path, which is defined by the following:
  1. Right views
  2. Right thought
  3. Right speech
  4. Right conduct
  5. Right vocation
  6. Right effort
  7. Right awareness
  8. Right meditation

Buddhism teaches that by following the Eightfold Path, one may achieve enlightenment, release from the cycle of reincarnation, and extinction of the individual (nirvana). However, in Pure Land Buddhism (found within the Mahayana tradition), it is taught that a new existence in a heavenlike realm awaits those who achieve enlightenment. Some forms of Buddhism (generally known as Theravada Buddhism) teach that not everyone is capable of this. The Lotus Sutra, however, teaches that Buddhahood, or enlightenment, is obtainable by all, and the Buddha has provided helpers to offer guidance along the way.

These guides are called *bodhisattvas*. They are people from different eons who have achieved enlightenment with the help of the Buddha throughout the course of the ages. Rather than being released from the cycle of reincarnation, though, they have opted to make appearances in the illusory world to help guide others toward enlightenment. The Lotus Sutra ultimately teaches that enlightenment is a universal prospect and thereby establishes what is known as the greater vehicle (*Mahayana*), replacing the older vehicle (*Theravada*) to "salvation."

Note: There are a number of translations of The Lotus Sutra in print as well as on the Internet (e.g., see sacred-texts.com/bud/lotus/index.htm).

8

The Upanishads

Lesson Focus

The Upanishads are some of the most ancient of all sacred writings. They make up a large portion of the vast array of Hindu scriptures. Most important, they are, in contrast to the more devotional aspect of other Hindu writings, a window into some of the major philosophical undercurrents of India's national religion.

Opening Discussion

Hinduism isn't just India's religion. Wherever people who trace their ancestry to India migrate, they bring their religion (and culture) with them. Accordingly, there are a large number of Hindus in America. Ask the class if they have encountered Hinduism in America. Also ask the class if anyone knows the major ideas of Hindu thought. Quick Reference Page 8 at the back of this book and Lesson 4 in *One God, many gods* (cph.org, item 20-3406) provide additional information to help guide your discussion.

While Hinduism may be a rather exotic religion, much of its ideas have been adopted by Americans, even those who identify themselves as Christians. In 2009, *Newsweek* published the article "We Are All Hindus Now," arguing that while 76 percent of Americans identify themselves as Christians, about half of them believe in things such as reincarnation and the notion that all religions lead to the same final, eternal destination. These beliefs are, at their

core, Hindu beliefs.

The *Newsweek* article's title suggesting we are all Hindus is hyperbole meant to attract readers' attention. But it does raise some interesting points about the decline of Christianity in America. Ask the class what they think about such phenomena going on all around us. Follow up, if time permits, by asking how Christians might respond. You might draw the discussion to an end by pointing out that the world around us, and our desire to be faithful witnesses and defenders of the Christian faith in the midst of this world, inspired this class on religious texts.

Understanding the Upanishads

Distribute copies of Participant Page 8. It provides a concise summary of the core ideas of the Upanishads as they relate to the basics of Hinduism. For additional facts on Hinduism, provide copies of Quick Reference Page 8.

After students have had time to read the handout, ask and allow the class (individually or in small groups) to answer the following questions:

What are the Upanishads? (The Upanishads are some of the earliest and most authoritative of the plethora of Hindu scriptures. Comprised of at least two hundred texts written over the course of several centuries beginning sometime before the fifth century BC, they are the primary sources for philosophical Hinduism.)

What is the most important concept in the Upanishads that expresses the basic contours of Hindu thought? (Hinduism is best characterized as monistic and, at the same time, pantheistic. That is, it teaches that god is one and all, and all are one. The Upanishads put it this way: "Brahman alone is—nothing else is.")

What do you find surprising about what the Upanishads teach? (Answers will vary.)

Thinking about the Upanishads

After briefly discussing the Upanishads, ask students to read Romans 1:18–23. (See sacred-texts .com/hin/upan, or obtain a copy at your local library or bookstore.) How might this passage help us understand how the various religious ideas we encounter were formed?

There are many opinions about this passage. The basic point to emphasize is that God has revealed Himself in nature, and all people recognize in some small way there must be something beyond or before basic existence. Problems emerge when humans start explaining the hunch that there must be something more than what we experience with our senses. Unless our knowledge of God and especially His disposition toward us is informed by God Himself—via His special revelation—our religious ideas are bound to fail.

Hinduism is a good example of man's attempt to explain that which we can't truly understand. As odd or different as it is, Hinduism presents a set of ideas that seek to answer man's most basic religious impulses. Ask the class if they can find any idea or flaw in the teachings of the Upanishads that might be a starting point in Christian-Hindu conversation and will provide the Hindu with an alternative—and true—way of looking at God and the world.

Although an abundance of controversy exists about what possible common ground Christians and Hindus share, there really is no theological common ground. Yet, the anxiety we find in Hinduism over one's next stage after death might just be a good place for Christians to emphasize the common lot in life that we all share—we cannot, on the basis of our own merits, ideas, and so forth, ever be confident of our eternal destiny or salvation. Read Romans 3:22–24. Only the Gospel, the truth that God comes into our sin-filled situation and deals with it on the cross of Golgotha, offers any definitive answer to mankind's problem of sin.

Closing

Conclude the study with the following prayer or one of your own.

Heavenly Father, we are a sinful lot—all of us. Even so You make plain to us that You care for us. You sent Your Son as a sacrifice for our sin. And You did this for all to see in time and space on the cross at Calvary. We thank and praise You that You have given us faith to trust in this all-atoning sacrifice. Continue to work, through Your Holy Church, to bring liberating Good News to all people everywhere. Amen.

The Upanishads

The Upanishads are some of the earliest and most authoritative of the plethora of Hindu scriptures. Comprised of at least two hundred texts written over the course of several centuries beginning sometime before the fifth century BC, they are the primary sources for Vedanta or, what one might call, philosophical Hinduism.

Hinduism is usually defined as polytheistic. In fact, some Hindu writings explain that there are more than 330 million gods in the Hindu pantheon of gods. Vedanta Hinduism, however, is best characterized as monistic and, at the same time, pantheistic. That is, it teaches that god is one and all, and all are one. The Upanishads put it this way: Brahman alone is—nothing else is.

What is Brahman? It is difficult to define and the Upanishads acknowledge this. "Different is [Brahman] from the known. . . . He truly knows Brahman who knows him as beyond knowledge; he who thinks that he knows, knows not. The ignorant think that Brahman is known, but the wise know him to be beyond knowledge." Yet, this realization is one of the goals of Vedanta Hinduism.

In Hindu thought, the world of autonomous physical and mental entities is an illusion (*maya*) superimposed on the world by our ignorance of ultimate reality. Only when we accept this fact can we really know the truth of the matter. Once such a state of consciousness is achieved, one can declare along with the Upanishads, "I am Brahman, self-luminous, the brightest treasure. . . . I am immortal, imperishable."

Until this point, the souls of every living thing (the *Atman*) are caught up in an endless cycle of reincarnation called *samsara*. The station (or *caste*) in life and physical body one inhabits in each incarnation is determined by the forces of karma. In other words, behavior and attitudes determine the nature of one's existence at any point along the cycle of *samsara*. The goal is to eventually be released (*moksha*) from this endless cycle. This can only be achieved by the realization that one is, in a sense, a sleeping deity and, moreover, essentially connected to all other things. That is, Brahman and Atman are one and the same.

Note: There are a number of translations of the Upanishads in print as well as on the Internet (e.g., see sacred-texts.com/hin/upan).

9

The Bhagavad Gita

Lesson Focus

The Bhagavad Gita is perhaps one of the most popular of the Upanishads. Not only does it reinforce much of what was covered in the previous study on the Upanishads, but it also goes into greater length on the Hindu view of the world in which we live—a world Hindus believe isn't truly real. Perhaps the most important reason to be aware of the Bhagavad Gita is that it is the primary scriptural text of the Hare Krishnas.

Opening Discussion

It used to be that Hare Krishnas were everywhere in larger cities. You would often see them in airports offering—in exchange for a donation—flowers and literature. That's not necessarily the case today. They are certainly still around, but they blend in much more than they once did. Nevertheless, chances are that someone in your class has had some sort of encounter with a devotee of Krishna Consciousness. Begin by asking about his or her experience. Alternatively, if no one has had any significant contact with a Hare Krishna, simply ask the class what they think of when they hear the term *Hare Krishna*. For additional information on Hare Krishna, provide copies of Quick Reference Page 9.

Understanding the Bhagavad Gita

Distribute copies of Participant Page 9. It provides a concise summary of the core ideas of the Bhagavad Gita. After students have had time to read the handout, ask and allow the class (individually or in small groups) to answer the following basic questions:

What is the Bhagavad Gita? (The Bhagavad Gita is sometimes regarded as the most important of the Upanishads. The text purports to describe a dialogue between Krishna and a legendary hero named Arjuna during a war named the Kurukshetra War.)

What are some of the ideas that the Bhagavad Gita illustrates about Hare Krishna? (It illustrates the ethical implications of the Hindu/Hare Krishna claim that the world we perceive is not truly real. If what we see and experience is only an illusion, then even categories of right and wrong and actions that are largely regarded as good or bad are of no value.)

What do you find surprising about the teachings in the Bhagavad Gita? (Accept all reasonable answers.)

What are the various yoga practices outlined in the Bhagavad Gita? For what are they used? (Raga yoga focuses on meditation. Karma yoga involves the practice of acting in an excellent manner in whatever you do. Jnana yoga includes the pursuit of knowledge. Bhakti yoga involves the practice of devotion.)

Thinking about the Bhagavad Gita

There is much one could discuss regarding the Bhagavad Gita. (See sacred-texts.com/hin/gita, or obtain a copy at your local library or bookstore.) This study focuses on the denial of moral realism (that there is a certain standard of morality that really does exist) and, to a lesser degree, the works orientation of Hinduism/Hare Krishna. The first is a focus because it is often assumed Hinduism is moralistic. It is not; nor is any other type of moral relativism.

Lead a discussion about the problems associated with the rejection of set moral standards. What

problems does it pose for the relationships between men and women? What problems does it pose for the Hare Krishna coming to terms with his or her failure to fulfill the basic precepts of the moral law before God—the moral Lawgiver?

The problems are numerous, of course. With regard to the former, there is no sense of objective moral standards. In what theologians regard as the civil realm, this leads to moral chaos, where everyone chooses his or her own moral code according to his or her own whims. With regard to the latter, if there is no moral standard given by a holy and just God, then the need for redemption is a moot issue. In other words, the Gospel does not make sense in the Hindu frame of reference. Of course, in a Hare Krishna context, salvation or, more accurately, self-realization is the result of men and women working to this end.

Read John 17:14–19. What do these words of Jesus say about the concept of moral relativism versus truth? (The devil and the world do not want us to hear the truth; there is a moral absolute and that absolute is found only in the Word of God.) Read the rest of the High Priestly Prayer from John 17:20–26. What beautiful assurance and promise do we read in these words? (Christ prays for all who believe in Him as Lord and Savior through the Word of God. He truly desires all believers to spend eternity with Him in heaven.)

Closing

Conclude the study with the following prayer or one of your own.

Heavenly Father, in Your mercy You gave us faith and thereby imputed the righteousness of Your Son to us. We thank and praise You for this. Keep us from worldly philosophies, and in the face of them, strengthen us to contend for the truth of what You accomplished through Jesus. Amen.

The Bhagavad Gita

The Bhagavad Gita is sometimes regarded as the most important of the Upanishads. It is a foundational text for members of the International Society of Krishna Consciousness (ISKCON), or Hare Krishna, and is regarded as the product of revelation from the Hindu god Krishna. No one knows when its seven hundred verses were actually written or who the author or transcriber was.

The text purports to describe a dialogue between Krishna and a legendary Hindu hero named Arjuna during a war named the Kurukshetra War, which—like its authorship—is unverifiable. The dialogue begins with Arjuna's uneasiness in slaying his opponents, particularly his cousins and friends who were nevertheless fighting against him. Krishna begins by teaching Arjuna his duties as a military leader.

Krishna also schools him—and other named observers in the text—in Hindu philosophy. Arjuna should not be troubled by the bloodshed he has caused. According to Krishna, Arjuna should realize that everything he is experiencing is an illusion. This was no reason to cease fighting. Rather, he instructs Arjuna to be indifferent to the violence he has witnessed and is, himself, largely responsible for. "When your intellect has cleared itself of its delusions, you will become indifferent to the results of all action, present or future."

The indifference to what most would regard as real events with real consequences is further amplified by Krishna when he exhorts Arjuna with the following: "He whose mind dwells beyond attachment, untainted by ego, no act shall bind him with any bond. Though he slay these thousands he is no slayer."

This illustrates well the ethical implications of the Hindu claim that the world we perceive is not real. If what we see and experience is only an illusion, then even categories of right and wrong and actions that are largely regarded as good or bad are of no value. They aren't actually real. They are, in fact, to be transcended. According to another Upanishad, when a person has obtained the right consciousness and realization of Brahman, he or she is freed from categories of, and will transcend, good and evil as he or she is united with Brahman.

The Bhagavad Gita also provides practical advice for achieving self-realization, and thereby union with Brahman, through four types of yoga. Raga yoga or meditation is one of them. Karma yoga or the practice of acting in an excellent manner in whatever you do is another. Jnana yoga, the pursuit of knowledge, and Bhakti yoga, the practice of devotion, comprise the other two. Practicing one or a combination of any of the four benefits a person in his or her path toward the realization of essential connection to ultimate reality—Brahman.

Note: There are a number of translations of the Bhagavad Gita in print as well as on the Internet (e.g., see sacred-texts.com/hin/gita).

10

The Book of Mormon

Lesson Focus

The Book of Mormon is the earliest and one of Mormonism's most-definitive books. It adds a different dimension to the life and ministry of Jesus by supposedly describing His activity on the American continent. Its theology—though more subtle than what one finds in *Doctrines and Covenants* and *The Pearl of Great Price*—likewise adds to the teachings of the historical (and biblical) Jesus. (See *One God, many gods,* Lesson 9.) The result is not a different Christian denomination but a radical reenvisioning of the person and work of Jesus, as well as the nature of Christianity that ultimately claims to clean up the errors that have crept into the Church since its formative period. The challenge that Mormonism poses to historic Christianity and the growing misperception that Mormonism is, in fact, Christian, warrant study of the Book of Mormon. In addition, Christians routinely bump up against Mormons and thus have opportunities to speak the true Gospel to them. Quick Reference Page 10 provides a snapshot of the Church of Jesus Christ of Latter-day Saints (Mormonism) for participants.

Opening Discussion

The Book of Mormon is nothing short of radical. It posits an entirely new understanding of Jesus. He is viewed as the off-spring of two deities—a heavenly father and mother—and spirit brother of Lucifer and the rest of the human race. In addition, he is reported to have ministered to ancient people living in America who are also believed to be descendants of the Jews.

Ask the class if they have heard this description of Jesus be-fore. Chances are they have, perhaps in their own home as they entertained Mormon missionaries. What is the problem with this story? (There are a number [e.g., it doesn't correspond with the biblical text, contradicts biblical theology, etc.], but you will want to focus on the fact that this alleged episode in ancient American history has no evidence to support its claims.)

Ask students who have had some interaction with Mormon-ism how Mormons explain this new history of Jesus. Most often they quote another Mormon text, *Doctrine and Covenants*, to explain it. Chapter 9:7–9 of that book explains that people can know that the story of Jesus coming to America and all of Mor-mon theology is true, not because it corresponds to the histori-cal record, but because they have experienced a burning in their bosom causing them to "feel that it is right." Discuss with the class the problems associated with such an epistemology (theory of knowledge). (Our feelings change from day-to-day; there is no objective position from which to develop a clear basis for teaching and doctrine.)

Understanding the Book of Mormon

Distribute copies of Participant Page 10. It provides a concise summary of the core story of the Book of Mormon. After students have had time to read the handout, ask and allow the class (indi-vidually or in small groups) to answer the following questions:

What is the significance of the Book of Mormon to Mormon-ism? (The Book of Mormon is the oldest Mormon text. According to Mormon legend, it contains a translation of a text originally inscribed in reformed Egyptian hieroglyph-ics on golden tablets.)

What does the Book of Mormon teach? (It claims to contain the lost history of two ancient American civilizations—the Jaredites and the descendants of Lehi and Nephi.)

What did you find especially surprising about its teachings? (Answers will vary. Most of what is taught concerning the history of these two ancient civilizations has no basis in verifiable history.)

Thinking about the Book of Mormon

It is baffling why people continue to believe the Book of Mormon and its account of the Jews coming to ancient America, despite the lack of any evidence. (For more information, see sacred-texts.com/mor/index.htm, or obtain a copy at your local library or bookstore.) This testifies to the grip Satan has on the hearts and minds of humans.

Have selected students read 1 John 4:1; 1 Thessalonians 5:21; and 2 Timothy 3:15 aloud, and discuss how these passages relate to the success of Mormonism. The Book of 1 John enjoins Christians to test the spirits. Ask the class where the teachings found in the Book of Mormon fall in their test of the spirits. Can Mormonism be described in any way as Christian? (No. The teachings of the Book of Mormon cannot hold up under scrutiny.)

Christians aren't only called to examine and separate themselves from false teachings, but they are also called to defend the Christian faith. Have the class read and discuss 1 Peter 3:15. Then, ask how a Christian might respond and even defend the truthfulness of the Gospel as it has been confessed through the ages in, for example, the Apostles' Creed over against the claims of Mormons based on the Book of Mormon. There are a number of ways. Focus, however, on the historicity of the Gospel, for, as Paul said, it did not occur "in a corner" (Acts 26:26). In fact, the essential events all took place "under Pontius Pilate" in the historical record and can be verified.

Read Galatians 1:6–9. What does Paul say about any new gospel being preached by someone else? (Even if this word comes from an angel, it is to be cursed.) How does this Scripture directly address the contents of the Book of Mormon? (It was supposedly revealed by an angel to Joseph Smith. Based on these verses, we should recognize it as false teaching.)

Closing

Conclude the study with the following prayer or one of your own.

Heavenly Father, Your only-begotten Son came down from heaven and died for us and our salvation. All this was accomplished at a certain place and in a certain time at the cross of Calvary. We thank and praise You for calling us to this faith. Continue to use us to point others back to that one event, where Your love and mercy were made manifest for all to see. Amen.

The Book of Mormon

The Book of Mormon is one of the chief texts of Mormonism. It is, according to Mormon legend, a translation of a text that was originally inscribed in reformed Egyptian hieroglyphics (a language unknown to historians and linguists) on golden tablets.

The story goes that the soon-to-be designated Mormon prophet Joseph Smith (1805–44) was approached by an angel named Moroni, who had buried the tablets containing the writings of ancient American prophets centuries earlier. Moroni directed Smith to render the writings in English for the purpose of restoring the Church of Jesus Christ. Smith did this from 1827 to 1829 under unverifiable circumstances by looking at them and interpreting the text through some mysterious spectacles called Urim and Thummim.

The following year, the Book of Mormon, the earliest defining Mormon writing, was published. It claims to contain the lost history of two ancient American civilizations—the Jaredites and the descendants of Lehi and Nephi. The Jaredites, the elder of the two, settled on the American continent after they left the tower of Babel around, according to Mormon chronology, 2250 BC. However, upon their arrival in the Western Hemisphere, they grew corrupt, and all traces of them were wiped off the earth.

The second group left Jerusalem around 600 BC. After traveling overland from the region of the eastern Mediterranean Sea and passing through the Arabian Peninsula, they landed on the west coast of South America. Soon, however, they divided into two groups—the Nephites and the Lamanites.

The story continues by describing how Jesus—who is, in the Mormon view, the offspring of a conjugal union between a heavenly father and mother (like the rest of humanity) and spirit brother of Lucifer—appeared to the Nephites. He preached the Mormon gospel that,

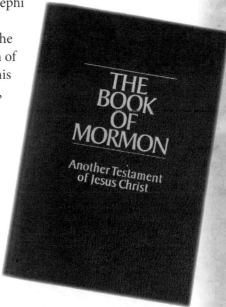

according to 2 Nephi 31:13–21, man must believe in the Mormon version of Jesus, repent of his sins, be baptized, receive the Holy Spirit through the laying on of hands, and then live a life of obedience.

Eventually, the Mormon story continues, the Nephites and their descendants became corrupt, and they disappeared from history. There is no historical record of a group of early Americans that fits the description of the Nephites as described by the Book of Mormon. Joseph Smith and the Church of Jesus Christ of Latter-day Saints, nevertheless, see themselves as the restorers of the pure gospel once delivered to the Nephites and corrupted by the Church for nearly two thousand years.

This historically undocumented group of ancient Americans became extinct in AD 421, when the Lamanites annihilated the Nephites at the battle of Cumorah. The Book of Mormon is seen by the Mormons to complement and correct the false theological interpretations of the Bible. It advances Mormonism's conviction that we (like Jesus and Lucifer) are all offspring of the heavenly father who are temporarily tested before returning to our primordial divine existence.

Note: The Book of Mormon is available at sacred-texts.com/mor/index.htm.

Participant Page 10 One Word, many writings
© 2012 Concordia Publishing House. Reproduced by permission. Photo: © Craig CozartIstockphoto.com.

11
The New World Translation

Lesson Focus

The New World Translation is the Bible of the Jehovah's Witnesses. Since its initial release, there have been more than 170 million copies (in a number of contemporary languages) printed, and there is no sign of its influence dwindling as Jehovah's Witnesses continue their proselytizing and publishing efforts.

Opening Discussion

Begin by asking students to discuss what they know about the Jehovah's Witnesses. You may want to consult Lesson 10 of *One God, many gods* (cph.org, item 20-3406) for points to discuss in more detail. Copies of Quick Reference Page 11 will provide participants with more information about the Jehovah's Witnesses.

Jehovah's Witnesses trace their roots back to a man named Charles T. Russell (1852–1916). After he separated from historic Christianity, he began to teach an alternative theology with heavy apocalyptic overtones that had just enough similarity to Christianity to appeal to a great many American Christians. Eventually, those who fell under the spell of Russell's teachings—especially as they were promoted by his successor, Joseph F. Rutherford (1869–1942)—officially formed the Jehovah's Witnesses cult.

Perhaps the greatest draw to this cult were the claims by Russell, Rutherford, and others, who claimed that they alone promoted a pure theology, unlike the mainline Christian churches, who were corrupted over the centuries with their distorted translations of the Bible. This claim was ultimately strengthened by the production of the New World Translation, which the organization claimed was a pure translation of the Bible from the original languages—but it was nothing of the sort.

Understanding the New World Translation

Distribute copies of Participant Page 11. It provides a concise summary of the basic issues surrounding the New World Translation, especially in relationship to some of the basic motifs of the Jehovah's Witnesses.

After students have had time to review the information, ask and allow the class to answer the following questions:

When and for what reason was the New World Translation first produced? (The translation was produced in the 1950s to correct the supposed errors found in previous biblical translations.)

Under what circumstances was it produced? What is peculiar about this "translation" of the Bible? (The church body has made every effort to keep secret the identity of the four translators. Former church leaders have revealed that none of the translators had formal training in the original biblical languages. True biblical scholars do not consider it a translation at all, but rather a reworking of existing translations.)

What are some of the theological problems of the New World Translation? (Because of various Jehovah's Witness teachings, certain terms or words, such as *hell* and *the cross*, are omitted from the translation. This book describes Jesus as a creation of God the Father rather than God's Son.)

Thinking about the New World Translation

After briefly discussing the New World Translation, ask students to discuss what they see as the primary problem with the translation. (Copies of the translation are available online at watchtower.org/e/bible/index.htm, or obtain a copy at your local library or bookstore.)

Its theological innovations are obviously problematic. The big issue, from which all the theological issues come, however, is the apparent process by which the New World Translation Bible was translated.

It is telling that the Watchtower organization (the parent organization behind the Jehovah's Witnesses) has kept secret the whole process and who was involved in the actual translating of the text. In fact, scholar after scholar has suggested that the biblical text was rendered into English to confirm and conform to the theology of the Jehovah's Witnesses rather than letting the biblical text inform their theology.

Jehovah's Witnesses claim to hold a high view of Scripture. Ask the class if this seems to be true based on the facts concerning the translation. What sort of argument could be made to illustrate that they do not? What warning does Paul offer in Colossians 2:8? (Their approach is deceitful, the very thing we are warned against.)

In short, Jehovah's Witnesses start with a particular theology and then impose it on the text. What are the problems associated with this approach? Read 2 Peter 3:14–19. (This approach denies the power of Scripture to speak for itself.)

Read 2 Timothy 3:15–17 and discuss the true purpose of Scripture. (Scripture points to the Savior, Jesus Christ. It trains us in all the things we need in life.)

If time allows, ask students to read the introductory matter of their Bible translation. Have them report to the group on the background of the text: Who is behind the translation? What people were involved? (The Preface to the English Standard Version says, "Each word and phrase in the ESV has been carefully weighed against the original Hebrew, Aramaic, and Greek, to ensure the fullest accuracy . . . that seeks as far as possible to capture the precise wording of the original text and the personal style of each Bible writer" [*TLSB*, xv]. The Preface goes on to report that ESV translation involved more than a hundred people lead by a fourteen-member Translation Oversight Committee. The publisher offers to share the complete list of translators and committee members with the reader.) How does this information compare to what you have learned about the New World Translation of the Holy Scriptures? (As with most accurate translations, it is the complete opposite of the secrecy surrounding the New World Translation.)

Closing

Conclude the study with the following prayer or one of your own.

Dear heavenly Father, You have called us all by the Holy Spirit so that we might enjoy eternal life with You. We ask for Your continual protection from all false teachings that would snatch us from Your grace. Give us the courage and conviction to address cults and other heterodox church bodies with the truth of the Gospel. Amen.

The New World Translation

In 1950, the Watchtower Bible and Tract Society announced that it was releasing a new translation of the New Testament. The reason: existing translations contradicted the "sacred truths which Jehovah God ha[d] restored to his devoted people." Thus, to ensure the Bible supported the theology of the leadership and people comprising the Jehovah's Witness sect, they decided to "translate" it anew. The result was the publication of the New World Translation of the Bible (the Old Testament would be published, too, by 1960).

From that day until the present, The Watchtower organization has kept the identities of the four translators a secret. There is a telling reason for this. None of them, as has been disclosed by former officials of the sect, had any academic training in the original languages of the Bible (Greek, Hebrew, and Aramaic). In fact, biblical scholars have time and again pointed out the mistranslations contained in the New World Translation. The general scholarly consensus is that it is not really a translation at all. Instead, the New World Translation is simple reworking of previously existing translations in order to conform to a theology which developed independent of any serious reflection on the biblical text.

Following are two examples of this. First, Jehovah's Witnesses believe that Jesus secretly returned to earth in 1914. So wherever Jesus' "coming" (parousia) is mentioned in the Greek New Testament, the New World Translation renders it "presence" (for he is already here). Second—and perhaps the most notorious forcing of the text into the theological assumptions of the Jehovah's Witnesses—is the New World Translation's rendering of John 1:1. Whereas the Greek text equates Jesus with God, the New World Translation reduces Him to "a god," that is, in Jehovah's Witness theology, the first creature that God made, but not God the Son who

does and has existed for all eternity with the Father and the Holy Spirit.

There are, of course, other examples. Because Jehovah's Witnesses do not believe hell exists, the New World Translation makes no mention of it, though there are four words and a number of places in the New Testament that describe such a place. Jesus' crucifixion on a cross—a brutal, historic fact from the first century AD—is described as taking place on a "torture stake." These and many more alterations and innovations are introduced in the translation, but are all placed there to support a theology developed apart from the text itself.

Note: The New World Translation of the Bible is available online at watchtower.org/e/bible/index.htm.

Participant Page 11 One Word, many writings
© 2012 Concordia Publishing House. Reproduced by permission. Photo: © Presniakov Olekdandr/Shutterstock, Inc..

12

Dianetics

Lesson Focus

L. Ron Hubbard's *Dianetics: The Modern Science of Mental Health* is just one of the source texts of Scientology. It is also probably the most prominent, as it in large part set this popular cult in motion. While no proponent of Scientology would call it sacred scripture, it does contain the cult's basic myths and ideological motifs.

Opening Discussion

Scientology used to capture a lot of media attention. Lately, this is not the case, but it is not due to its decline in popularity. Indeed, Scientology is still quite popular in various locations across the United States, but it is not discussed as much in the media these days because it has become part of the American cultural landscape.

For this study, begin by asking students what they know of Scientology. You may want to consult Lesson 11 of *One God, many gods* (cph.org, item 20-3406) to aid in classroom discussion. Quick Reference Page 12 provides additional information about Scientology for participants. After giving students opportunity to share their thoughts, explain the basic point of Scientology: at the root of it is the assumption that humans are essentially god-like in nature and extraterrestrial in origin. They just have not realized it. Humans have been so distracted and confused about who they really are by what scientologists call *engrams*—negative views of one's self—that they have forgotten this. There is a way toward self-realization, however. Scientology teaches that humans can, through a rather expensive process of auditing (as well as attending seminars), come to terms with their *thetan* (essentially spiritual) nature.

Understanding Dianetics

Distribute copies of Participant Page 12. It provides a concise summary of the background and ideas found in *Dianetics*.

After students have had time to read the handout, direct students or small groups to answer the following questions:

When and by whom was *Dianetics* written? (The book was first published in 1950, by L. Ron Hubbard, whose previous experience involved writing science fiction novels.)

Of what religious tradition is it a part? (Dianetics is the sourcebook for the Church of Scientology. A number of celebrities follow Scientology, including Tom Cruise and John Travolta.)

Why did L. Ron Hubbard write *Dianetics*? (Hubbard himself reports that he was looking for a way to get rich; he spoke about starting his own religion as a means to that goal.)

What are some of the main ideas of *Dianetics*? (We cannot truly perceive reality; our mind is blocked by an accumulation of false memories.)

What do you find surprising about what is taught in *Dianetics*? (Answers will vary. Participants may mention some of the unusual practices of Scientology's auditing members as they attempt to attain higher levels of existence.)

Thinking about Dianetics

After briefly discussing *Dianetics* (you may wish to obtain a copy at your local library or bookstore), have students discuss: Why would anyone believe what this book teaches? (Allow students to share their opinions. Sadly, the devil leads people away from the true God by leading them to false beliefs like those found in *Dianetics*.)

Have students read 1 Timothy 4:1 and 1 John 2:18. What do these verses say about the nature of false beliefs? (In the last days, even Christians will be enticed by demonic forces to forsake the truth. How much easier must it be for a person with no connection to the truth to believe in falsehoods as preposterous as Scientology!)

Have students read Ephesians 6:12. How does this passage help us come to terms with the nature of our struggle with false beliefs? (While there is much in the realm of ideas to be dealt with, our struggle in the world and against false beliefs is ultimately a struggle against the devil.)

Life and our interaction with false beliefs and religion must therefore be attended to with prayer.

Closing

Conclude the study with the following prayer or one of your own.

Dear heavenly Father, keep us ever steadfast in the one true faith. Be with us, strengthen and encourage us, as we remain in the world as light amidst the darkness. Amen.

Dianetics

Dianetics: The Modern Science of Mental Health is the chief text of Scientology. Its author, L. Ron Hubbard (1911–86), indicated in the 1940s that he wanted to get rich. The way to do that was not by writing science fiction (as he had been doing), but, as he remarked on a number of occasions, to start a new religion. He published this work in 1950 and launched the Church of Scientology.

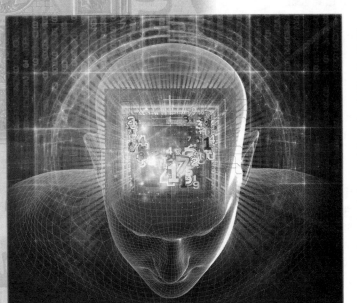

Though the book is difficult to understand, particularly if one expects a lucid and coherent text, its main ideas can be discerned. They seem to revolve around what Hubbard saw as our generally false perceptions of reality. This is due to what *Dianetics* refers to the reactive mind's unwitting collection of false memories (*engrams*) that, as they build up, lead one to believe they are real.

This causes a mental illness of sorts. The solution to this is a process of clarification of what is truly real, known as dianetic auditing. These audits—in seminars and therapeutic sessions that cost a fairly large amount of money—help one suppress and eventually deactivate the reactive mind, so that what is termed the analytical mind can emerge free from the false perceptions that have been collected over time.

Such a person will eventually become what *Dianetics* refers to as a *Clear*—a person with superior intellect and ethics as well as superior mental and physical health. Such people, Hubbard stated the same year he published *Dianetics*, would become the world's new elite and ruling class.

One of the peculiar things about Hubbard's *Dianetics* is that it seems pretentiously scientific. Appearances, however, can be deceiving. In fact, the deeper one investigates Scientology, the more it becomes clear that this is a cult, dressed up in quasi-scientific assertions and underpinned by New Age mysticism. (See Hugh B. Urban, *The Church of Scientology*). Nevertheless, it constitutes a fairly well-represented movement in America's religious landscape.

Note: Dianetics does not appear to be available online, but can be checked out at your local library or purchased online.

Participant Page 12 One Word, many writings
© 2012 Concordia Publishing House. Reproduced by permission. Photo: © Shutterstock, Inc.

Quick Reference Pages

Use the reproducible Quick Reference Pages that follow for concise information regarding the religious groups whose sacred writings are discussed in *One Word, many writings.* The Web sites listed on each of these pages were active at the time of publication. Concordia Publishing House is not responsible for the content of these sites, nor does it endorse them. The Ontario (Canada) Consultants on Religious Tolerance provides an excellent general Web site on world religions at religioustolerance.org.

Judaism

History

Judaism traces its roots back to Abraham in 2000 BC. God's promises to Abraham (Genesis 12:1–3) and His covenant with him (Genesis 15:1–21) begin the relationship between God and the Jews.

Central Teaching

God is a personal, all-powerful, eternal, and compassionate God. His history with His people and His basic teachings are found in the *Torah*, the first five books of the Old Testament. Judaism also accepts as true the entire Old Testament and the *Talmud*, a twenty-seven-hundred-page record of the teachings of ancient rabbis.

Significant People

In addition to Abraham, the other Old Testament patriarchs are considered giants of the faith. King David also is revered because he led Israel to become a mighty world power.

Today's Connection

There are almost six million Jews living in the United States. Almost every major city has at least one synagogue.

Christian Response

Most Jews will be familiar with Jesus, but they won't acknowledge Him as the Savior. Because of their belief that the Messiah has not yet come, we can witness to Jews by celebrating the hope we have in Jesus. An active, dynamic faith that openly confesses Jesus is the best witness.

Web Resource

jewfaq.org/index.htm

Christianity

History

The Christian Church dates its beginning from Pentecost in AD 33. The Church was essentially one body for a thousand years. A split between the East and West in 1054, the Reformation movement in the sixteenth century, and other divisions in the past five hundred years have resulted in hundreds of denominations today.

Central Teaching

Christians recognize Jesus to be the Christ (the Anointed One or Messiah) sent by God to redeem all people from sin. Jesus is both God and man (Colossians 2:9; Isaiah 9:6; 2 John 7). Any religion that does not acknowledge Jesus as Lord and Savior is not Christian (1 John 4:1–6).

Significant People

Jesus' disciples were twelve chosen men and included Peter, James, John, and others.

Paul converted to Christianity about five years after Jesus' resurrection and brought Christianity to people throughout the Roman empire.

Martin Luther (1483–1546) preached that we are justified by grace alone, through faith in Christ alone, as taught by Scripture alone.

Today's Connection

About one third of the world's population describes themselves as Christian. Though there are many denominations, the Church is united in belief in the triune God, the Bible as God's Word, and salvation through Jesus.

Christian Response

Central to the Christian faith is the belief that Jesus, God's only Son, is both fully human and fully divine. He suffered, died, and rose again so that we might receive God's gift of forgiveness of sins. Jesus fulfilled the Law so that we might receive God's gift of Christ's righteousness.

© 2008 Concordia Publishing House. Reproduced by permission. Photo: © Shutterstock, Inc.

Islam

History

In AD 610, a businessman named Muhammad (c. 570–632), in Mecca in Saudi Arabia, began to preach submission to the one God, Allah. He did this as a result of a vision of the angel Gabriel, who gave him the Qur'an, Islam's sacred scriptures. Today, Islam is the religion of about 21 percent of the world's population.

Central Teaching

The central confession in Islam is the *shahada*, "There is no God but Allah, and Muhammad is his prophet." *Muslim* means "one who submits." Islam teaches submission to God in all things. It is a code of honor, a system of law, and a way of life based on the Qur'an. The level of devotion to the moral code determines one's salvation.

Significant People

Muhammad, the founder of Islam, is considered Allah's last and greatest prophet. Muslims also believe that Abraham, Moses, and Jesus are great prophets. Jesus is not considered to be God's Son or the Messiah.

Today's Connection

Islam is the world's fastest-growing religion. Some experts have predicted that the number of Muslims will surpass the number of Christians as early as the year 2025. Islam is especially active on college campuses and in large communities.

Christian Response

The important Christian teaching to keep in mind when encountering Islam is that Jesus is not just a prophet: He is the Son of God, Savior of the world, and God's promised Messiah, who died on the cross for the forgiveness of our sins.

Web Resource

islamworld.net

Confucianism and Taoism

History

Confucianism and Taoism both emerged in ancient China. Around 500 BC, various feudal lords were locked in political and military conflict. This is known as the period of the Warring States. In the aftermath of the turmoil, many people began to ask how China could become reunited. Solutions were proposed by hundreds of intellectuals during the period of the Hundred Schools.

Central Teaching

Confucius claimed that harmony with the *Tao* (way or path) was best attained by restoring order in society. Confucianism sees the family as the bedrock of society. Therefore, proper relationships at home between children, parents, grandparents, and even deceased ancestors (by veneration) needed to be instituted.

Lao Zu (Laozi) focused not on society but on nature. Nature, he taught, contained five elements—metal, earth, wood, fire, and water—and was empowered by two energies: *yin* (male) and *yang* (female). Harmony with the Tao and even immortality could be achieved by balancing the elements and energies.

Significant People

By far the two most influential thinkers were Confucius and Lao Zu. They both taught in their respective writings—The Analects of Confucius and the Tao te Ching (Dao de Jing)—that the only way for society to recover from the political and sociocultural devastation of the Warring States period was for Chinese society to realign itself with the Tao in which the universe was moving.

Today's Connection

Today many Chinese embrace the teachings of Confucius as their ethical code of conduct and the mysterious notions of Taoism in their private, meditative life. How many is unclear, but these teachings are surely also to be found throughout the large population of Asian Americans.

Christian Response

Confucianism and Taoism both fall into the trap of worshiping the creation rather than the Creator. As Christians, we acknowledge Jesus Christ as Lord and Savior and that salvation can be found only through His death and resurrection.

Web Resource

daoiststudies.org
interfaith.org/confucianism

Buddhism

History

Buddhism arose in India about 500 BC. Siddhartha Gautama found that his Hindu beliefs did not adequately explain the suffering and pain he observed in the world. Through religious contemplation, Gautama became Buddha, "the enlightened one," and taught his discoveries.

Central Teaching

Pure Buddhism is more philosophy than religion, a godless pietism. Other forms of Buddhism revere Buddha as a deity and speak of salvation through faith in him. Buddhism is a journey to an enlightened state of being. People do this by accepting the Four Noble Truths and following the Eightfold Path.

Significant People

Buddhism was founded by Siddhartha Gautama (Buddha) about 563–483 BC. Other major teachers include Nichiren, AD 1222–82 in Japan, and the Dalai Lama, currently living in exile from Tibet in Dharamsala, India.

Today's Connection

Buddhism has gained popularity among media and sports celebrities worldwide. The middle road and balanced life of Buddhism are a welcome change from a celebrity life. Today, followers number over three hundred million worldwide, including between two and five million in the United States.

Christian Response

Salvation is not achieved by right thoughts and right things. It is a gift given to us by a personal God through the sacrifice of His Son. We receive this gift by faith.

Web Resource

buddhanet.net

Hinduism

History

One of the world's oldest religions, Hinduism developed between 1800–1000 BC in India. Hinduism contains many sects. Hinduism is both a religion and a way of life. It is described in the Vedas (considered the world's most ancient scriptures, about 1000 BC) and the Bhagavad Gita, an eighteen-chapter poem.

Central Teaching

Hindus believe that all things are part of God, that souls are reincarnated at death, and that our lives are influenced by *karma* (good and bad actions in this life determine one's status in the next). The goal is *moksha*, release from *samsara* (the cycle of reincarnation), to become one with God.

Significant People

Hinduism developed over many centuries; there is no single significant founder or leader. The most famous among its followers is Mahatma Gandhi, who led India to freedom from the British Empire in the early-twentieth century.

Today's Connection

The New Age movement and Transcendental Meditation are popular movements founded in Hinduism. Meditation and yoga have become common forms of stress release in our society, with classes offered at local fitness and community centers.

Christian Response

According to God's Word, salvation is found only in the saving work of the triune God (Acts 4:12). Although Christians are to live in obedience to God, their salvation is not dependent on their obedience (Ephesians 2:8–9).

Web Resource

uwacadweb.uwyo.edu/religionet/er/hinduism/index.htm

Hare Krishna

History

In 1965, Srila Prabhupada (1896–1977) arrived in New York City on a mission to propagate Gaudiya Vaishnavism, a form of Hinduism. In 1966, he established the International Society for Krishna Consciousness (ISKCON), commonly known as the Hare Krishna movement. Under his guidance, the Society grew to a worldwide confederation of more than one hundred *asramas*, schools, temples, institutes, and farm communities.

Central Teaching

Krishna explains all the essential spiritual truths: the difference between the soul and the body, the difference between the soul and the Supreme Soul (god), the science of reincarnation, the nature of time, the ultimate goal of yoga, why different kinds of religion appeal to different kinds of people, and the ultimate purpose of human life.

Significant People

Srila Prabhupada wrote a commentary on the Bhagavad Gita. George Harrison, Ringo Starr, and John Lennon—all former members of The Beatles—have used Hare Krishna chants at various times in their musical recordings.

Today's Connection

The regular release of *Back to Godhead* magazine provides Hare Krishna followers with answers to all types of questions. We also see a strong connection between Hare Krishna, meditation, and some types of yoga practices. Many people looking to improve themselves and find answers to the questions in their lives have been drawn to Hare Krishna. Followers of Hare Krishna are strictly vegetarian; yet they must also avoid onions, garlic, leeks, and similar vegetables.

Christian Response

There is no historical evidence for the battle central to the teachings in the Bhagavad Gita. The moral relativism of this movement and followers' willingness to respect all people's beliefs make it very difficult for the Christian to witness to Hare Krishnas.

Web Resource

harekrishna.com

Quick Reference Page 9 One Word, many writings
© 2008 Concordia Publishing House. Reproduced by permission. Photo: © Shutterstock, Inc.

Mormonism
The Church of Jesus Christ of Latter-day Saints

History

The Church of Jesus Christ of Latter-day Saints was formed by Joseph Smith, Jr. in 1830 in Fayette, New York. Smith claims to have translated the Book of Mormon from golden tablets entrusted to him by the angel Moroni. In 1844, Smith and his brother were imprisoned and killed. Brigham Young moved the group to the Salt Lake Valley in Utah, where it flourished.

Central Teaching

Mormons believe that God was once a human being just as we are and that we can become gods and earn admittance to a celestial heaven.

Significant People

In addition to Joseph Smith (1805–44) and Brigham Young, other important leaders include Oliver Cowdery, who figured prominently in the founding, and Sidney Rigdon, an early convert and theologian in the Latter-day Saints who was passed over for leadership at Smith's death.

Today's Connection

Mormon tabernacles have been erected in all parts of the United States and are planned or under construction on all major continents. Mormon membership has grown to more than thirteen million members worldwide with more than five million in the United States. The sight of two young men in business suits and black nametags riding bicycles and knocking on people's doors is familiar to many. These are among the more than fifty thousand volunteer missionaries who serve the church each year.

Christian Response

Christians bear witness to the one triune God, through whom we have salvation by God's grace alone, not by our efforts. The Bible is God's unchanging truth and our only authority for teaching.

Web Resource

mormon.org/mormonorg/eng

Jehovah's Witnesses

History

Charles T. Russell (1852–1916) founded The Watch Tower Bible and Tract Society in Pennsylvania in 1884. The group became officially known as Jehovah's Witnesses in 1931. The Witnesses claim worldwide membership of nearly seven million, with approximately one million members in the United States.

Central Teaching

Jehovah's Witnesses believe that they have been organized to announce the early establishment of God's rule on earth. The Witnesses use the Watchtower organization to interpret the Bible and as the main means for spreading their doctrine. They also have their own version of the Bible called the New World Translation.

Significant People

Charles T. Russell was the founder of the group and author of most of the Studies in the Scriptures, a series that outlines the group's teachings. His successor, Joseph Rutherford, moved the organization to Brooklyn, New York, and established the governing body, a small group of men who continue to direct the work and determine the teachings of the Witnesses.

Today's Connection

It seems likely that most everyone will encounter Jehovah's Witnesses at their own doorstep at some time or another. Door-to-door witnessing is the only activity of members on which records are kept and is the most important requirement for their salvation.

Christian Response

Christians can share three important truths with the Witnesses: (1) the Bible is the only source for all knowledge about God and His plan for salvation; (2) salvation is not earned by good works, but is ours by God's grace through faith in Jesus Christ; and (3) Jesus Christ is true God, and all who believe in Him have forgiveness of sins and eternal life.

Web Resource

watchtower.org

Quick Reference Page 11 One Word, many writings © 2008 Concordia Publishing House. Reproduced by permission. Photo: © Presniakov Olekdandr/Shutterstock, Inc.

Scientology

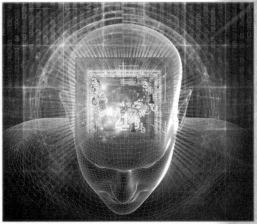

History

Scientology was founded in 1954 by L. Ron Hubbard. The movement began with the popularity of Hubbard's self-help book, *Dianetics: The Modern Science of Mental Health*.

Central Teaching

Using the methods of Scientology, people are capable of raising their own spiritual awareness to the point of achieving immortality. Those who reach this level are called *operating thetans* (thay-tns).

Significant People

Scientology is based solely on the many writings of L. Ron Hubbard. Among the members of the Church of Scientology are numerous celebrities, including John Travolta, Tom Cruise, Kirstie Alley, and Lisa Marie Presley.

Today's Connection

L. Ron Hubbard's writings are widely available in bookstores. *Dianetics*, his most famous title, is widely marketed as a self-help book. Scientology benefits from endorsements, donations, and public appearances from its celebrity members.

Christian Response

Thanks be to God that, as Christians, we do not have to rely on ourselves for salvation! In our Baptism, we are claimed by God "who saved us and called us to a holy calling, not because of our works, but because of His own purpose and grace" (2 Timothy 1:9).

Web Resource

scientology.org

Photo Credits